INSPECTOR GENERAL
DEPARTMENT OF DEFENSE
400 ARMY NAVY DRIVE
ARLINGTON, VIRGINIA 22202–4704

I0407876

August 25, 2004

MEMORANDUM FOR DIRECTOR, DEFENSE THREAT REDUCTION AGENCY

SUBJECT: Report on Contracts Awarded by the Defense Threat Reduction Agency in Support of the Cooperative Threat Reduction Program (Report No. D-2004-111)

We are providing this report for information and use. We considered management comments on a draft of this report in preparing the final report. The Defense Threat Reduction Agency comments conformed to the requirements of DoD Directive 7650.3, additional comments are not required.

We appreciate the courtesies extended to the staff. Questions should be directed to either Mr. Timothy E. Moore at (703) 604-9282 (DSN 664-9282) or Mr. Terry L. McKinney at (703) 604-9288 (DSN 664-9288). See Appendix D for the report distribution. The team members are listed inside the back cover.

By direction of the Deputy Inspector General for Auditing:

David K. Steensma
Assistant Inspector General
for Contract Management

Office of the Inspector General of the Department of Defense

Report No. D-2004-111   **August 25, 2004**
   (Project No. D2003CF-0183)

Contracts Awarded by the Defense Threat Reduction Agency in Support of the Cooperative Threat Reduction Program

Executive Summary

Who Should Read This Report and Why? This report should be read by DoD contracting officials, program managers, and budgeting officials that work together to plan, award, administer, and fund task orders awarded through multiple contracts. This report addresses the significance of providing fair opportunity to all contractors involved in a multiple-award contract and the importance of Agency-wide directives to create internal controls for managing the award of task orders under multiple-award contracts.

Background. Congress established the Cooperative Threat Reduction Program in December 1991 to assist the countries of the former Soviet Union in destroying and reducing the proliferation of nuclear, chemical, and biological weapons of mass destruction. In September 2001, to accomplish the Cooperative Threat Reduction Program goals, the Defense Threat Reduction Agency (DTRA) awarded five contracts to five different contractors under a multiple-award solicitation. The total estimated dollar value of the five Cooperative Threat Reduction integrating contracts was $5 billion. In FYs 2002 and 2003, DTRA awarded 32 task orders under the integrating contracts worth approximately $415.8 million. These task orders required such tasks as building or improvement of transportation infrastructure including roads and railbeds, the construction of buildings, the destruction of weapons, and the clean up of the destruction site.

Results. DTRA has used the multiple-award process to efficiently streamline Cooperative Threat Reduction Program procurements. The Federal Acquisition Regulation requires that when multiple award orders are awarded, contracting officials must give each contractor a fair opportunity to be considered for each order or cite an exception to fair opportunity. On three task orders for subsequent phases of multiphased requirements, DTRA used a contractor down-select process[*] that did not provide each contractor supporting the Cooperative Threat Reduction Program fair opportunity to be considered for the task orders and did not cite an exception to the fair opportunity requirement. Using these procedures, DTRA awarded orders valued at over $78 million without providing fair opportunity or citing an exception. The task orders represented subsequent phases of three projects with a combined value over $262 million. As a result, the task orders may not have been awarded to the best value contractor and continued use of the process will result in more awards without the benefits of

---

[*] The down-select process is a process in which the program office evaluates all the estimated costs and summary work plans submitted by multiple contractors that outline the concept and approach to satisfy the technical and performance requirements of the Government for a task order. Based on criteria that was provided to the contractors, the program office then selects one contractor to receive the task order. The down-selected contractor must submit a full technical and cost proposal.

competition. In addition, DTRA included a 5-year award-term incentive in the Cooperative Threat Reduction multiple-award contracts, creating a probable 10-year period of performance. Although the 5-year award-term is allowed by the Federal Acquisition Regulation, the five current contractors supporting the Cooperative Threat Reduction Program will be the only integrating contractors working on the Cooperative Threat Reduction Program until year 2011. The Cooperative Threat Reduction program is expected to last until 2016 and 55 contractors had expressed interest in the program prior to the award of the current integrating contracts. The result of the multiphase project contractor selection procedures and the 5-year award term incentive is the creation of a limited competition environment where the current contractors supporting the Cooperative Threat Reduction Program will obtain such a competitive advantage that other contractors will be unable to compete for future contracts. (Finding A)

With the exception of providing fair opportunity on multiphase requirements, DTRA generally complied with applicable laws and regulations when awarding contract task orders under the Cooperative Threat Reduction integrating contracts. Although the contracting process was well documented in procurement negotiation memorandums, poor management controls on contract documentation that cut across DTRA directorates resulted in data and documentation discrepancies for 26 of 32 contract actions reviewed. Specifically, of the 32 contract task orders reviewed we found 2 contained incorrect accounting and appropriation data; 11 contained incomplete technical evaluations regarding contractor proposed labor hours; 4 contained incomplete documentation regarding subcontractor costs, indirect rates, or other direct costs; and 20 lacked justification for the type of contract used. (Finding B)

The Director, DTRA should implement policy that mandates that contracting officials either provide fair opportunity or document the rationale for an exception for each task order awarded; ensure that future contract performance periods do not restrict competition; and finalize the Cooperative Threat Reduction Integrating Contract Business Processes and Associated Responsibilities guidance document to make certain that multiple-award contract documentation contains data and justification that comply with the guidance when making contracting decisions. See the findings for the detailed recommendations.

We reviewed the management control program as it related to the task orders awarded under the Cooperative Threat Reduction integrating contracts in support of the Cooperative Threat Reduction Program. Management controls did not ensure that contractors were provided a fair opportunity on multiphase tasks and that the accounting and appropriation data were correct.

Management Comments. The Acting Director, Defense Threat Reduction Agency concurred with the recommendations and initiated corrective actions; therefore no further comments are required. The acting director agreed to compete future task orders or document the rationale for a fair opportunity exception if the task orders are not competed. In addition, the acting director agreed to direct more attention towards improving documentation that would assist in avoiding erroneous accounting and appropriation data on contract actions; and to ensure that negotiated labor hours, subcontractor pricing, indirect rates, and other direct cost be fully supported and explained. Finally, the acting director concurred with the need to document the justification for contract type selection. See the Finding section of the report for a discussion of management comments and the Management Comments section of the report for the complete text of the comments.

Table of Contents

Background

Defense Threat Reduction Agency. The Defense Threat Reduction Agency (DTRA) was established in October 1998 to reduce the threat to the United States and its allies from nuclear, biological, and chemical weapons of mass destruction (WMD). DTRA operates under the authority, direction, and control of the Under Secretary of Defense for Acquisition, Technology, and Logistics. DoD provides resources and technical assistance to countries of the former Soviet Union through umbrella agreements. The umbrella agreement with Russia, signed on June 7, 1992, establishes the overall framework under which the U.S. provides assistance to Russia.

Cooperative Threat Reduction Program. Congress established the Cooperative Threat Reduction (CTR) Program in December 1991 to assist the countries of the former Soviet Union in destroying and reducing the proliferation of nuclear, chemical, and biological WMD. Prior to October 1998, the Defense Nuclear Agency, which became the Defense Special Weapons Agency in June 1995, managed CTR projects. Currently, DTRA manages the day-to-day operations of the CTR Program. Between FYs 1992 and 2003, Congress appropriated $5.1 billion to DoD, the designated CTR executive agent for the CTR Program. As of September 2003, the CTR Program had successfully eliminated over 6,100 warheads, 100 bombers, 1,800 ballistic missiles (includes silos, launchers, and submarines), and 190 nuclear tunnels.

CTR Integrating Contracts. In September 2001, DTRA awarded five indefinite delivery/indefinite quantity (ID/IQ) contracts from a multiple-award solicitation to accomplish the CTR Program goals. Task orders awarded under the CTR integrating contracts are often for large, complex projects that may include various tasks such as the building or improvement of transportation infrastructure including roads and railbeds, the construction of buildings, the destruction of weapons, and the clean up of the destruction site. In many instances, integrating contractors manage and perform oversight of Russian subcontractors, although Russian subcontractors handle the technical functions of the projects. The awarded contracts cover a 5-year period with a term award incentive based on contractor performance for a 5-year contract extension. The estimated dollar value of the five multiple-award contracts totals $5 billion. As of April 26, 2004, task orders valued at $434.1 million have been awarded using the CTR integrating contracts. Table 1 lists the five CTR integrating contractors and their respective awarded contract numbers.

1

Table 1. CTR Integrating Contracts Multiple-Award Contractors

Contractor	Contract No.
Parsons Delaware, Inc.	DTRA01-01-D-0010
Bechtel National, Inc.	DTRA01-01-D-0011
Washington Group International, Inc.	DTRA01-01-D-0012
Raytheon Technical Services Company	DTRA01-01-D-0013
Brown & Root Services, A Division of Halliburton International, Inc.	DTRA01-01-D-0014

Before the establishment of the CTR integrating contracts, DTRA awarded contracts directly to Russian contractors, which often resulted in an abundance of logistical perplexities. The average length of time to award contracts to Russian contractors ranged between 10 and 12 months. In addition, manpower and travel expenses were extensive. By awarding the CTR integrating contracts, DTRA created a dedicated team of technically qualified contractors who would compete among themselves for task orders, thereby saving resources and time.

Task Order Awards. DTRA uses a streamlined approach to select contractors for task order awards under the CTR integrating contracts. Under this approach, the DTRA program office posts the description of a project on the internet using the program application Docushare to allow the five multiple-award contractors the opportunity to review the proposed project. DTRA requests that the contractors submit top-level work plans showing how the contractor would complete the project. The top-level work plans contain rough order of magnitude cost estimates for completing the projects. The program office then selects one contractor for the task order award, based primarily on the technical solution and abilities of the contractor as delineated in the top-level work plan.

Objectives

Our overall audit objective was to determine whether DTRA contracting processes in support of the CTR Program complied with applicable laws and regulations. Specifically, we determined whether contracts were awarded and managed to ensure the Government received best value in cost and contractor performance. We also reviewed the management control program as it related to the overall audit objective. See Appendix A for a discussion of the scope and methodology and the review of the management control program and Appendix B for prior coverage.

A. Competition of Task Orders

DTRA used the multiple-award process to efficiently streamline CTR procurements. However, DTRA awarded three task orders worth over $78 million that did not comply with Federal Acquisition Regulation (FAR) ordering requirements, and DTRA provided multiple-award contractors a probable 10-year contract term, thereby, limiting future competition. DTRA contracting officials used a contractor down-select process[1] when issuing task orders for subsequent phases of multiphased projects that did not provide each contractor supporting the CTR Program a fair opportunity to be considered for the task orders and did not cite an exception to the fair opportunity requirement. As a result, task orders may not have been awarded to the best value contractor and continued use of the multiphase ordering process will result in more awards without the benefits of competition. In addition, DTRA is developing a limited competition environment in which a single contractor will have the experience and established infrastructure necessary for performing specific weapons destruction tasks that, in effect, void future competition on task orders for threat reduction efforts.

Criteria

Multiple-award contracts are regulated by FAR Part 16, "Types of Contract." Ordering procedures are regulated by FAR Subpart 16.505, "Ordering." The CTR integrating contracts are composed of five indefinite delivery/indefinite quantity (ID/IQ) contracts. An ID/IQ contract provides for an indefinite quantity, within stated limits, of supplies or services during a fixed period. The Government issues orders under the contracts for individual requirements. FAR Subpart 16.504(c)(1) states that contracting officers must, to the maximum extent practicable, give preference to making multiple awards of ID/IQ contracts under a single solicitation for the same or similar supplies or services. A multiple award situation allows qualified contractors the opportunity to compete with each other for orders.

Fair Opportunity. FAR 16.505(b)(1)(i) requires that when a multiple-award task order valued over $2,500[2] is awarded, contracting officials must provide each contractor a fair opportunity to be considered for the award or cite one of four exceptions to fair opportunity. The four exceptions are:

- the agency need for the supplies or services is so urgent that providing a fair opportunity would result in unacceptable delays,

---

[1] The down-select process is a process in which the program office evaluates all the estimated costs and summary work plans submitted by multiple contractors that outline the concept and approach to satisfy the technical and performance requirements of the Government for a task order. Based on criteria that was provided to the contractors, the program office then selects one contractor to receive the task order. The down-selected contractor must submit a full technical and cost proposal.

[2] Section 803 of the FY 2002 National Defense Authorization Act, as implemented in Defense FAR Supplement 216.505-70, increased the $2,500 amount to $100,000 for services contracts.

- only one awardee is capable of providing the supplies or services required at the level of quality required because the supplies or services ordered are unique or highly specialized,

- the order must be issued on a sole-source basis in the interest of economy and efficiency as a logical follow-on to an order already issued under the contract, provided that all awardees were given a fair opportunity to be considered for the original order, and

- it is necessary to place an order to satisfy a minimum guarantee.

Multiphased Approaches. According to FAR Subpart 16.505(b)(1)(iii), the contracting officer can use a multiphased approach when developing ordering placement procedures:

> . . . when effort required to respond to a potential order may be resource intensive (e.g., requirements are complex or need additional development), where all contractors are initially considered on price considerations (e.g., rough estimates), and other considerations as appropriate (e.g., proposed conceptual approach, past performance). The contractors most likely to submit the highest value solutions are then selected for one-on-one sessions with the Government to increase their understanding of the requirements, provide suggestions for refining requirements, and discuss risk reduction measures.

Award Term. The "award term" incentive is modeled after the award fee incentive described in FAR Subpart 16.405-2. Instead of rewarding a contractor for excellent performance with additional fee, an award-term incentive rewards a contractor by extending the contract period of performance without a new competition. The Government monitors and evaluates the performance of a contractor and if the Government decides that the performance of the contractor was excellent, the contractor earns an extension.

Streamlined Selection of Contractors

To provide fair opportunity to all five multiple-award contractors, DTRA program offices post a task order requirements package on Docushare when a new project will be awarded. The task order requirements package includes a statement of objectives representing the overall scope of the task as currently understood. DTRA requests that the CTR integrating contractors submit top-level work plans showing how the contractor would complete the project. The contractors, if interested in performing the task, provide top-level work plans containing executive summaries of their technical and management approaches and rough order of magnitude cost estimates for completing the projects.

At the time that the top-level work plans and rough order of magnitude cost estimates are developed, the requirements to perform the projects have not been fully developed and may change significantly when statements of work are developed. Changes due to revised policy guidance, shifts in project priorities, or unknown site conditions may cause the resulting task order to differ from what was proposed by the contractor.

The program office selects one contractor for the task order award, referred to as the down-select decision, based primarily on the technical solution and abilities of the contractor as delineated in the top-level work plan. Government experts work with the selected contractor to develop the statement of work. The selected contractor is then required to submit full technical and cost proposals, which are evaluated in a sole-source environment using an Integrated Product Team (IPT) to determine the negotiation position of the Government.

Task Orders for Multiphased Requirements

DTRA used a multiphased approach for larger requirements that could not be fully defined at the time of initial award. When using a multiphased approach, DTRA awarded a task order for the initial phase of the project to the contractor down-selected on the basis of its top-level work plan and rough order of magnitude cost estimate. DTRA included a clause in multiphase projects that stated:

> The contractor was down-selected with the expectation of negotiating and performing all phases of the task order requirements package (TORP). . . . Notwithstanding the Government's intent to award all phases to the selected contractor, the Government reserves the right to recompete and/or award any remaining phases to another source, if it is determined to be in the Government's best interest to do so.

The multiphased approach was developed to help mitigate the risks associated with the instability of project requirements that take place in the former Soviet Union when projects can be directly affected by foreign Government decisions or other unforeseen problems. Many CTR projects do not develop as originally envisioned.

Of 32 task orders reviewed, 4 were for a subsequent phase of a multiphased project. DTRA contracting officials awarded three task orders to the contractor who performed Phase 1 of the multiphase effort without providing each contractor a fair opportunity to be considered or citing one of the exceptions to fair opportunity. The fourth task order cited the urgency exception to fair opportunity. The estimated value of the three orders was over $78 million. However, the three orders represented phases of task order requirements packages worth over $262 million. The initial down-select decisions were based on top-level work plans including rough order of magnitude cost estimates that were submitted by contractors interested in meeting the entire multiphase requirement. The contractors understood that the down-selected contractor would be awarded the entire effort, but each phase would be on a separate task order. Although only four task orders have been awarded using the multiphased approach, this process will lead to the majority of CTR task orders being awarded without fair opportunity in future years. The FAR does not provide the multiphased approach as a method to make a task order award, therefore, there should be a separate down-select process for each phase of a DTRA project or an exception to fair opportunity should be cited.

Multiphased Projects. DTRA contracting officials did not comply with FAR Part 16 fair opportunity requirements when they awarded the three task orders. DTRA contracting officials contended that fair opportunity had been provided based on the top-level work plans for the task order requirements package. The officials also contended that the FAR provides the contracting officer broad discretion in developing order placement procedures and that the DTRA procedures were developed using broad discretion. However, because of the uncertainty of the CTR requirements and the potential for changes to occur after the down-select decision, the best value contractor for the task order requirements package may not be the best value contractor for each individual phase of the project. Had DTRA provided each contractor a fair opportunity to be considered for each task order, best value awards would be documented whether significant changes to the project had occurred.

Contract DTRA01-01-D-0011, Task Order Requirements Package 0051. Task order requirements package 0051, "SS-25 Intercontinental Ballistic Missile Base Elimination," represented a multiphase project with an estimated value of $80 million. Task Order No. 8 under contract DTRA01-01-D-0011, valued at $1.4 million, was issued to Bechtel National, Incorporated, for Phase I of the requirement to eliminate up to nine Strategic Rocket Force SS-25 Road Mobile Intercontinental Ballistic Missile bases located throughout Russia. Phase I established the baseline processes and procedures to eliminate SS-25 Road Mobile Missile Bases by regiment. Task Order No. 9, valued at $13.7 million, was issued to Bechtel National, Incorporated, for Phase II of the requirement. The purpose of Phase II was to eliminate five regiments of SS-25 Road Mobile Intercontinental Ballistic Missiles. Bechtel National, Incorporated, was selected to perform Phase II without providing a fair opportunity to the other CTR contractors or citing one of the fair opportunity exceptions. DTRA selected Bechtel National, Incorporated, when Task Order No. 8 was awarded. However, documentation in the contract file for Task Order No. 9 stated that competition for this order was accomplished during the down-select process for the entire requirement. The DTRA contracting officials contended that competition was accomplished for the entire requirement during the Task Order No. 8 down-select process and that there was no need to cite a fair opportunity exception when issuing Task Order No. 9.

Contract DTRA01-01-D-0012, Task Order Requirements Package 0072. Task order requirements package 0072, "SS-25 Storage Facility Construction and Burn Stand Renovation," represented a multiphase project with an estimated value of $53.4 million. The overall requirement was to build sufficient missile storage to enable the closing of Strategic Rocket Forces missile bases hosting the SS-25 Road Mobile Intercontinental Ballistic Missile. Task Order No. 3 under contract DTRA01-01-D-0012, valued at $3.2 million, was issued to Washington Group International for Phase I of the requirement, to determine the site of the missile storage buildings and missile storage infrastructure and the design of the infrastructure. DTRA contracting officials awarded Task Order No. 9, valued at $49.5 million, to Washington Group

International for Phase IV of the requirement, which was to provide for the construction of storage facilities in Perm, Russia, for SS-24/SS-25 loaded motor cases and for renovating and equipping the motor burn facility at Kemerovo, Russia. They issued the task order without providing a fair opportunity to the other CTR contractors or citing one of the fair opportunity exceptions. DTRA selected Washington Group International when Task Order No. 3 was awarded. However, the DTRA contracting officials contended that competition was accomplished for the entire requirement during the Task Order No. 3 down-select process and that there was no need to cite a fair opportunity exception when issuing Task Order No. 9.

Contract DTRA01-01-D-0013, Task Order Requirements Package 0071. Task order requirements package 0071, "SS-25 Integrated Missile and Launcher Elimination," represented a multiphase project with an estimated value of $128.8 million. The overall requirement was to decommission and eliminate SS-25 Intercontinental Ballistic Missiles and their road-mobile launchers, demilitarize certain vehicles, and remove solid propellant from missile motors. The entire project, consisting of four phases, was awarded to Raytheon Technical Services Company based on a top-level work plan and rough order of magnitude cost estimate. Task Order No. 8, under contract DTRA01-01-D-0013, valued at $3.9 million, was issued to Raytheon Technical Services Company for Phase I of the requirement, which was for planning, licensing, and design. DTRA contracting officials then awarded Task Order No. 12, valued at $14.9 million, to Raytheon for Phase II which was for renovation, including renovation and certification for operation of the SS-25 missile disassembly and elimination facilities and equipment at Russian corporation, Votkinsky Zavod and at the Piban'shur Intercontinental Ballistic Missile dismantlement facility. They awarded Task Order No. 12 without providing fair opportunity to the other CTR contractors or citing an exception to fair opportunity. The DTRA chief of policy stated in an e-mail dated December 24, 2002, that DTRA did not need to cite an exception if Phase II was awarded to the same contractor who performed Phase I. The e-mail stated, "Phasing does not require an exception to fair opportunity as long as we stay with the down-selected contractor. If we shift to another source we're back at square one-early strategy session, etc."

Award-Term Incentive

The CTR integrating contracts all included a 5-year award-term incentive. The contracts stated that the initial 5-year contract period may be unilaterally extended based on contractor performance. If the award-term incentive was exercised, a 5-year extension would be issued, resulting in a total contract term of 10 years from the date of the original award. The FAR, however, discourages the use of contracts that last longer than 5 years. FAR 17.204(e) states that the total of the basic and option periods of a service contract shall not exceed 5 years unless otherwise approved in accordance with agency procedures. Although this does not specifically address award-term incentives, it does indicate that contracts extending beyond 5 years are not preferred. This 5-year contract limit was made mandatory on March 23, 2004, when DoD published an interim rule in the Federal Register "Contract Period for Task and Delivery Order Contracts" (Defense Federal Acquisition Regulation Supplement Case 2003-D097). The rule established a 5-year limitation on the contract period for a task order or delivery order contract awarded by DoD under the authority of Section 2304a, title 10, United States Code. The rule implements Section 843 of the National Defense Authorization Act for FY 2004 (Public Law 108-136).

The award-term incentive restricts competition in the CTR Program. The CTR integrating contracts were awarded in 2001. Because the contracts included the award-term incentive, the five CTR integrating contractors will likely be the only contractors performing work on the CTR Program until 2011. Therefore, the Government will be limited to the current five CTR integrating contract contractors during the entire 10-year contract term. In addition, the experience gained by these contractors and the infrastructure that is established while performing the weapons of mass destruction tasks over a 10-year period may eliminate other contractors from competing for future contracts. The incumbent contractors supporting CTR Program will have a great advantage based on their 10 years of experience which will be a deterrent to other contractors in competing for future CTR Program contracts.

It is also noteworthy that one of the contractors supporting the CTR Program stated that it may soon cease participating in the CTR Program due to lack of success of the contractor in the fair opportunity process for the award of task orders. DTRA stated that if any of the current CTR integrating contractors drops out of the program after the first 5 years, DTRA will continue with the program until 2011 with the remaining contractors. Therefore, the CTR Program may have fewer than five contractors available to work during the second 5-year term of the CTR integrating contracts, further limiting the competitive process.

Fair Opportunity Requirements

FAR Requirements. DTRA contracting officials did not correctly interpret the FAR requirements regarding fair opportunity. The DTRA officials awarded three task orders for subsequent phases of requirements without providing each contractor a fair opportunity to be considered for the award or citing one of the four exceptions to fair opportunity. DTRA contracting officials contended that basing a down-select decision on top-level work plans covering the entire project satisfied fair opportunity requirements for all subsequent task orders. This interpretation was incorrect because the FAR requires that contracting officials provide fair opportunity for each individual task order or cite an exception to fair opportunity. This position was also maintained by the Government Accountability Office (GAO) in a recent report. In GAO Legal Report B-302499, "The Federal Acquisition Streamlining Act of 1994 – Fair opportunity procedures under multiple award task order contract," July 21, 2004, the GAO ruled that the Federal Acquisition Streamlining Act:

> does not permit an agency to choose between issuing a requirement to a pre-selected contractor or opening the requirement to all multiple-award contractors. Rather, FASA [the Federal Acquisition Streamlining Act] mandates that all contractors be given a fair opportunity to be considered for every task order unless a statutory exception applies.

Changes to project requirements occurring after the down-select decision further support the need for providing fair opportunity on all task orders involving phased projects. Such changes to requirements may render the initial down-select decision invalid for the initial task order as well as the subsequent phases of the requirement, because the initial down-select decision was potentially based on different requirements. Dealing with the former Soviet Union creates much uncertainty with project requirements, frequently resulting in changes to requirements that can impact the basis on which the down-select decision was made.

For example, Bechtel National, Incorporated, was down-selected to perform all the work for task order requirements package 0051, "SS-25 Base Elimination Program." Initially, DTRA contracting strategy was to award a single CTR integrating contract task order for the overall project. The integrating contract task order was to be structured as a base task order for the effort for the first year with annual priced options for the remaining 8 years. A streamlined competition was held among the CTR integrating contractors resulting in Bechtel National, Incorporated, being down-selected to perform the entire project. Prior to the initiation of the task order, the Russians decided to change the requirement from an SS-25 base-by-base elimination to an SS-25 regiment-by-regiment elimination. Each base consists of two to five regiments. Eliminating a regiment of a Russian Federation military unit consists of the infrastructure and fixed structures for nine SS-25 missiles and launchers, along with the transportation of the missiles off-site to a storage location and the launchers to an elimination facility. As a result of these changes, DTRA officials decided to execute task order requirements package 0051 in phases with separate task orders issued for each phase. The DTRA officials acknowledged that the regiment-by-regiment approach might extend the project until 2016 and add some cost to the overall project by requiring the contractor to return to a base several times. DTRA contracting officials did not think the change was significant to the scope of the project, and they felt that the down-select decision would not have been altered. Although this may be the case, the changes to the requirement seem significant enough to have warranted providing the other CTR contractors a fair opportunity to provide a more efficient solution to the requirement. At a minimum, the changed requirements should have warranted providing fair opportunity on subsequent phased task orders unless an exception to fair opportunity was cited and justified.

Decision to Use Award-Term Incentives

DTRA contracting officials stated that they included the 5-year award-term incentive in the CTR integrating contracts to provide incentives to enhance contractor performance. However, as previously stated, FAR 17.204 discouraged the use of contracts for periods over 5 years, and the March 23, 2004, interim rule in the Federal Register now mandates that contract periods will be limited to 5 years. In addition, the award-term incentive was to be exercised based on the CTR integrating contract contractors' overall performances. Therefore, the award-term incentive did not provide significant motivation for exceptional contractor performance on any particular task.

Conclusions

Fair Opportunity. The DTRA practice of awarding task orders for subsequent phases of a project without providing each contractor supporting the CTR Program a fair opportunity to be considered for the task orders and not citing an exception to fair opportunity requirements creates the potential that task orders will not be awarded to the best-value contractor. It is possible that the contractor best suited to perform subsequent phases of a requirement is not the same contractor who was best suited to perform Phase I. Therefore, to ensure that the Government is receiving best value, DTRA should either provide fair opportunity for each task order awarded or should cite and justify one of the fair opportunity exceptions, if applicable, when awarding task orders for subsequent phases of a requirement.

Award-Term Incentive. The decision of the DTRA contracting officials to use the award-term incentive in the CTR integrating contracts precludes the Government from obtaining the competitive benefits of having additional contractors available to work during the second 5-year term of the contracts. Only the current CTR integrating contract contractors will be able to work on the CTR Program until 2011. The Government will not be able to obtain potential cost savings and other benefits available from additional competition.

The use of the award-term incentive creates the potential for a future sole-source environment in the CTR Program. Prior to the award of the current CTR integrating contracts, 55 other contractors expressed interest in the program. As more time passes with the current CTR integrating contracts, the contractors working on the CTR Program become the only contractors with the experience and infrastructure to perform weapons destruction tasks in the former Soviet Union and it becomes more difficult for other contractors to compete with them, ultimately eliminating other contractors from future competition. For these reasons, and the fact that the new interim rule in the Federal Register limits contract periods of performance to a maximum of 5 years, we recommend that DTRA not include 5-year award-term incentives in future multiple award procurements. DTRA should award new contracts using full-and-open competition no less often than every 5 years.

Management Comments on the Finding

Management Comments. The Acting Director, Defense Threat Reduction Agency was pleased that we found that DTRA effectively used the multiple-award process to efficiently streamline CTR Program procurements. The acting director believes that competing entire projects among all the CTR integrating contractors, then systematically and logically issuing separate orders to the successful contractor for integral project phases represents a prudent business approach by DTRA. The DTRA process mitigates project risk by requiring former Soviet Union subcontractors to complete their portion of each project prior to moving to the next phase of the project and providing an exit strategy from a project if problems arise. Although noted in the draft report, CTR integrating contracts award-term provisions (which were included as an incentive for the contractors) were allowable at the time of the CTR integrating contracts awards and were not in violation of the FAR.

Recommendations, Management Comments, and Audit Response

A. We recommend that the Director, Defense Threat Reduction Agency:

1. Either provide all contractors working under the Cooperative Threat Reduction integrating contract a fair opportunity to be considered for the award of all task orders issued under the Cooperative Threat Reduction integrating contracts or document the rational for an exception to fair opportunity, if applicable, including task orders issued for subsequent phases of multi phased projects.

Management Comments. The Acting Director, Defense Threat Reduction Agency concurred. The acting director stated that although the DTRA down-select process was developed under the broad discretion granted to contracting officers by the FAR Part 16.5, DTRA acknowledges that the FAR Subpart 16.505(b)(2) requires that, for all orders over $2,500, every multiple Indefinite Delivery/Indefinite Quantity awardee must be given a fair opportunity to compete or an exception to fair opportunity must be documented. DTRA will either compete or document the rationale for the exception for all future Cooperative Threat Reduction Integrating Contractor task orders.

2. Award all future Cooperative Threat Reduction procurement contracts with performance periods that do not restrict competition.

Management Comments. The Acting Director, Defense Threat Reduction Agency agreed that the award-term provisions contained in the Cooperative Threat Reduction Integrating Contracts contributed to limiting the competitive environment, however, the acting director stated that she did not consider issues on the limits of competition as serious as the draft report suggested. The acting director stated that DTRA retains the right to award Cooperative Threat Reduction projects to other contractors if circumstances warrant and have done so when such awards were in the best interest of the Government.

Audit Response. A combination of not competing multiphase projects and excessively long award-term provisions would create a noncompetitive environment. However, actions taken by DTRA in response to Recommendation 1. and recent changes in the FAR have alleviated our concerns. Defense Threat Reduction Agency comments are considered responsive. Further comments by DTRA are not required.

B. Contract Documentation

With the exception of providing fair opportunity on multiphase requirements, DTRA generally complied with applicable laws and regulations in awarding task orders under the CTR integrating contracts. Although the contracting process was well documented in procurement negotiation memorandums, poor management controls on contract documentation that cut across DTRA directorates resulted in data and documentation discrepancies for 26 of 32 contract actions reviewed. Specifically, of the 32 contract task orders reviewed:

- 2 contained incorrect accounting and appropriation data;

- 11 contained incomplete technical evaluations regarding contractor proposed labor hours;

- 4 contained incomplete documentation regarding subcontractor costs, indirect rates, or other direct costs; and

- 20 lacked justification for the type of contract used.

DTRA needs to improve management controls to better ensure that all contracts have correct accounting and appropriation data and contain adequate documentation. If controls are not improved, contract accounting and appropriation data will not be properly accounted for and decisions of the contracting officers cannot be substantiated.

Contracting Requirements

FAR 15.404(e)(2) states that at a minimum, the technical analysis should examine the types and quantities of material proposed and the need for the type and quantities of labor hours and the labor mix.

FAR 16.103(d) states that each contract file shall include documentation to show why the particular contract type was selected.

FAR 16.505(b)(1)(ii)(e) states that the contracting officer must consider price or cost under each order as one of the factors in the selection decision.

Contract Task Order Problems

Of the 32 contract task orders reviewed in support of the CTR Program, 26 had at least one documentation-related problem. The following table summarizes problems found during the audit. Appendix C provides the contract numbers of the contracts with documentation related problems.

Table 2. Summary of Problems Found

Problem Areas	Occurrences/Universe	Percent
Incorrect Accounting and Appropriation Data	2/32	6
Inadequate Documentation Supporting Price Reasonableness Decision	15/32	47
Inadequate Explanation of the Type of Contract Used	20/32	63

Verification of Accounting and Appropriation Data. We identified two task orders awarded for work to be performed in Iraq that incorrectly included the accounting and appropriation data for work to be performed in the former Soviet Union. The orders were Task Order No. 10 of contract DTRA01-01-D-0013, valued at $1.2 million, and Task Order No. 4 of contract DTRA01-01-D-0014, valued at $1.4 million. The Office of the Secretary of Defense (Comptroller)/Chief Financial Officer confirmed that the appropriation data cited on the task order award were restricted to work performed in the former Soviet Union. When notified, DTRA comptroller officials immediately modified the task orders to replace the incorrect accounting and appropriation data. DTRA comptroller officials noted that there were no control procedures for the DTRA Contracting Division to verify accounting and appropriation data on task orders with the DTRA Comptroller Division.

Contract Documentation. Of 32 contract actions reviewed, 15 documented and supported the basis for determining that prices negotiated during the IPT process were fair and reasonable, 15 did not have supportive documentation, and 2 were for undefinitized contract actions[3]. For 11 of the 15 task orders without supportive documentation, technical evaluations did not address contractor proposed labor hours. The other four task orders did not discuss the subcontractor costs, concerns raised by the technical evaluation for contractor proposed labor hours, indirect rates, and other direct costs. Several previous Inspector General, DoD, audits have reported on similar problems with contract documentation. The two undefinitized contract actions were documented in accordance with the Defense FAR Supplement.

Price negotiation memorandums were usually detailed and showed that prime and subcontractor proposed costs including labor rates, material costs, and other costs had been reviewed. However, contracting officers did not detail the need for proposed labor hours. The technical evaluations that the contracting officers depended on for justification, routinely contained statements that proposed labor hours were reasonable. However, there was no basis for these determinations. Without an explanation of how labor hours were determined reasonable, we were unable to determine whether rationale of the contracting officer for determining

---

[3] An undefinitized contract action is any contract action where the contract terms, specifications, or price are not agreed upon before performance is begun under the action.

that prices paid were fair and reasonable. For example, for Task Order No. 1 of contract DTRA01-01-D-0013, the price negotiation memorandum states that the technical evaluation of the project manager included a review and approval of the number and type of labor hours proposed by the contractor in the technical proposal. However, the technical evaluation does not mention the number of labor hours proposed by the contractor. There were no official command directives or instructions detailing the information required from program offices. Normally, the program office is responsible for producing technical evaluations that contain a basis for the number of labor hours proposed.

Selection of Contract Type. For 20 task orders reviewed, contracting officials did not justify why the contract type selected was appropriate even when cost-type contracts were used. Although some of the task order files included a brief explanation of why a certain contract type was required, other task order files did not. In some instances, we questioned whether a cost-type contract was appropriate. For example, contracting officials selected a cost-plus-fixed-fee contract type for Task Order No. 8 of contract DTRA01-01-D-0011. There was no explanation in the task order file describing why this type of contract was selected. However, the contract price negotiation memorandum stated that requirements for Task Order No. 8 were well defined and that an independent Government cost estimate had not been developed primarily because of the DTRA Program Manager's familiarity with another Phase I requirement for similar services. Therefore, we could not determine whether the proper type of contract was selected and the Government was receiving the best value.

Defense Threat Reduction Agency Internal Controls

For DTRA to better ensure that all contracts have correct accounting and appropriation data and adequate documentation, they need to improve management controls.

Business Processes and Associated Responsibilities Guidance. In October 2003, DTRA developed the draft CTR Integrating Contract Business Processes and Associated Responsibilities guidance document that describes the process followed for initiating and coordinating Cooperative Threat procurement actions with emphasis on CTR integrating contract task order processes. As a command directive, this document can be used across the different DTRA business divisions and other directorates to strengthen internal controls within the Contracting Division.

Accounting and Appropriation Data Controls. DTRA comptroller officials review accounting and appropriation data when they receive a copy of awarded contract actions; however, internal control procedures are not in place to verify the data is correct before the contract action is signed. In Task Order No. 10 of contract DTRA01-01-D-0013 and Task Order No. 4 of contract DTRA01-01-D-0014, neither the comptroller or the contracting officials had an explanation why the wrong accounting and appropriation data had not been discovered before the contract action was signed by the contracting officer. Internal control procedures can alleviate potential for unintentional noncompliance with financial and regulatory requirements. Comptroller personnel should review all contract actions that obligate funds to ensure that correct accounting and appropriation data are used. The draft business processes guidance document does not mention controls for reviewing accounting and appropriation data, but this type of document could serve as an excellent vehicle for future controls.

Justification of Labor Hours. Technical evaluators are required by the FAR to explain the basis used for determining that proposed labor hours are reasonable. The draft business processes guidance document did not specifically state any reference to providing documentation in the contract files to justify contractor proposed labor hours. However, the guidance noted that regardless of the proposal method, full proposal or Integrated Product Team (IPT) approach, a government evaluation of the proposal must be properly documented. According to the guidance, the project manager leads the effort in the proposal evaluation. The project manager is responsible for the technical evaluation and ensures that the management and technical approaches of the contractor meet the requirements of the statement of objectives or statement of work. In 11 of the task orders we reviewed, the technical evaluations did not provide sufficient analysis of the proposed contractor labor hours. In the draft business processes guidance document, a draft format of a new price negotiation memorandum included a review of the number of labor hours and the labor hour mix as part of the analysis to determine fair and reasonable prices. DTRA management needs to ensure that program offices are aware of this requirement and contracting offices need to ensure the requirements are met before placing orders on CTR integrating contracts.

Contract Type Documentation. The FAR notes that each contract file must include documentation as to why a particular contract type was selected. According to the draft business processes guidance document, DTRA conducts an early strategy session in which the project manager presents an overview of the planned task order. If the task order supports the CTR Program, a contract type decision is made to award either a firm-fixed-price, cost-plus-fixed-fee, or cost-plus-award-fee contract. DTRA officials prepare a Memorandum for Record on the early strategy session proceedings. In some of the task order files reviewed, DTRA officials discussed in the Memorandum for Record the reasons why a particular type of contract was selected. However, in 20 orders reviewed there was no explanation in the contract task order files. Documentation of the early strategy session is an appropriate vehicle for DTRA contracting officials to document the justification of the contract type selected for task orders. DTRA contracting officers need to better document and support their rationale for choosing cost reimbursable contract types.

Management Controls. Although all DTRA directorates including the CTR Directorate and the Iraq Weapons Elimination Directorate are listed as assessable units in the DTRA management control program, the program is inadequate in addressing the problems identified during the audit because controls on multiple-award contracts are necessary that cut across directorates. In addition, DTRA management controls for verifying accounting and appropriation data were

15

not adequate. Adequate management controls will increase the likelihood that the Government is receiving the best value for its money and is conforming to financial statutory and regulatory requirements.

Conclusion

In general, DTRA is documenting and supporting its business decisions when awarding task orders under the multiple-award CTR integrating contracts. However, DTRA needs to focus more attention on internal management controls. Accounting and appropriation data on contract actions must be accurate and documentation of contract actions must meet all FAR requirements. Management controls that are supported by senior managers can achieve these goals.

Management Comments on the Finding

Management Comments. The Acting Director, Defense Threat Reduction Agency concurred with the finding. The acting director stated that DTRA has strengthened internal controls by placing additional oversight responsibility in the majority of directorates through the creation of a Senior Business Officer. DTRA also employs extensive and independent reviews by the Contracts Policy Oversight and Career Management Branch and the office of the General Counsel prior to the award of a task order to ensure compliance with all policies and regulations.

Recommendations

B. We recommend that the Director of the Defense Threat Reduction Agency establish and support management controls by completing and implementing the Cooperative Threat Reduction Integrating Contract Business Processes and Associated Responsibilities guidance document to direct:

1. Accounting and appropriation data is correct on all contract actions.

2. Program offices provide the Contracting Division technical evaluations that provide a basis for required labor hours on contract actions.

3. Contracting officers document the reasons for the selection of a particular contract type.

Management Comments. The Acting Director, Defense Threat Reduction Agency concurred with the recommendations and stated that the Cooperative Threat Reduction Integrating Contract Business Processes and Associated Responsibilities guidance document will be finalized and implemented over the next several months. The acting director stated that focusing more attention on improving documentation will help to avoid inclusion of erroneous accounting and appropriation data on contract actions. The acting director also concurred with the need for DTRA to focus more attention on improving documentation to ensure that negotiated labor hours, subcontractor pricing, indirect rates, and other direct costs are fully supported and explained. The acting director concurred with the need to focus additional attention on documenting the justification for the contract type selection.

Appendix A. Scope and Methodology

This audit was performed as a self initiated risk benefit assessment. Our review focused on task orders awarded under DTRA Cooperative Threat Reduction integrating contracts in support of the CTR Program. DTRA awarded the contracts on September 7, 2001. The contract actions reviewed covered FYs 2002 through 2003. We examined the individual task orders, top-level work plans, rough orders of magnitude, statements of work, Defense Contract Audit Agency reviews, price negotiation memorandums, technical evaluations, source selection decisions, and other miscellaneous correspondence. Our review covered five ID/IQ contracts with a combined estimated value of $5 billion and 32 task orders with an estimated value* of $415.8 million. Our audit included the following steps:

   1. The first step determined whether DTRA contracting officers provided each multiple-award contractor a fair opportunity to be considered when issuing task orders and whether contracting officers properly justified exceptions to the fair opportunity process.

   2. The second step determined whether DTRA contracting officers adequately documented and supported price reasonableness decisions. We reviewed price negotiation memorandums and documents supporting the information contained in the price negotiation memorandums.

   3. The third step determined whether DTRA contracting officers justified the use of the contract type selected when issuing task orders.

We interviewed DTRA contracting and program offices, including the DTRA acquisition executive and the head of the contracting activity. We also met with contractor officials and an official from the Office of the Secretary of Defense (Comptroller)/Chief Financial Officer. We performed this audit from August 2003 through May 2004 in accordance with generally accepted government auditing standards.

Limitations. We did not determine whether contracting officials performed adequate surveillance on cost-reimbursement contracts. It was determined that time constraints did not allow for a thorough examination of tasks being performed in the former Soviet Union.

Use of Computer-Processed Data. We did not use computer-processed data to perform this audit.

GAO High-Risk Area. GAO has identified several high-risk areas in DoD. This report provides coverage of the high-risk area to "Improve processes and controls to reduce contract risk."

---

* Estimated value represents the amount that contracting officials estimate as the value of the entire contract including all option years. If the term estimated value is not used, the dollar value will refer to the value of contract orders in effect at the time of the audit.

Management Control Program Review

DoD Directive 5010.38, "Management Control (MC) Program," August 26, 1996, and DoD Instruction 5010.40, "Management Control (MC) Program Procedures," August 28, 1996, require DoD organizations to implement a comprehensive system of management controls that provides reasonable assurance that programs are operating as intended and to evaluate the adequacy of the controls.

Scope of the Review of the Management Control Program. We reviewed the management control procedures related to task orders awarded under the CTR integrating multiple-award contracts in support of the CTR Program. We specifically reviewed the fair opportunity process and the accounting and appropriation data used. We reviewed management's self-evaluation applicable to these areas.

Adequacy of Management Controls. We identified material management control weaknesses for DTRA, as defined by DoD Instruction 5010.40. DTRA management controls for task orders awarded under the CTR integrating contracts in support of the CTR Program were not adequate for ensuring that contractors were provided a fair opportunity to be considered. Recommendation A.1., if implemented, will improve the process for providing contractors a fair opportunity to be considered. Also, DTRA management controls for verifying accounting and appropriation codes were not adequate. Recommendations B.1. through B.3., if implemented, will improve overall DTRA management controls for task orders awarded under multiple contracts. A copy of the report will be provided to the senior official responsible for management controls in the Defense Threat Reduction Agency.

Adequacy of Management's Self-Evaluation. DTRA officials did not establish management controls for multiple-award contracts that cut across directorates and, therefore, did not report on the material management control weaknesses identified by the audit.

Appendix B. Prior Coverage

During the last 5 years, GAO and the Inspector General of the Department of Defense (IG DoD) have issued 13 reports discussing the CTR Program. Unrestricted GAO reports can be accessed over the Internet at http://www.gao.gov. Unrestricted IG DoD reports can be accessed at http://www.dodig.osd.mil/audit/reports.

GAO

GAO Legal Report No. B-302499, "The Federal Acquisition Streamlining Act of 1994 – Fair opportunity procedures under multiple award task order contract," July 21, 2004

GAO Report No. GAO-03-1008R, "FY 2004 Annual Report on the Cooperative Threat Reduction Program," July 18, 2003

GAO Report No. GAO-03-627R, "FY 2003 Annual Report on the Cooperative Threat Reduction Program," April 8, 2003

GAO Report No. GAO-03-526T, "Weapons of Mass Destruction: Observations on U.S. Threat Reduction and Nonproliferation Programs in Russia," March 4, 2003

GAO Report No. GAO-03-341R, "Cooperative Threat Reduction Program Annual Report," December 2, 2002

GAO Report No. GAO-01-694, "Cooperative Threat Reduction: DoD Has Adequate Oversight of Assistance, but Procedural Limitations Remain," June 19, 2001

IG DoD

IG DoD Report No. D-2004-050, "Management Structure of the Cooperative Threat Reduction Program," February 5, 2004

IG DoD Report No. D-2004-039, "Cooperative Threat Reduction Construction Projects," December 18, 2003

IG DoD Report No. D-2003-131, "Cooperative Threat Reduction Program: Solid Rocket Motor Disposition Facility Project," September 11, 2003

IG DoD Report No. D-2002-154, "Cooperative Threat Reduction Program Liquid Propellant Disposition Project," September 30, 2002

IG DoD Report No. D-2002-033, "Management Costs Associated With the Defense Enterprise Fund," December 31, 2001

IG DoD (cont'd)

IG DoD Report No. D-2001-074, "Cooperative Threat Reduction Program," March 9, 2001

IG DoD Report No. D-2000-176, "Defense Enterprise Fund," August 15, 2000

Appendix C. Contract Task Order Problems

Table C-1. Task Orders with Inadequate Documentation

Item Number	Contract/Task Order Number	Contract Type
1	DTRA01-01-D-0011/0002	Cost-Plus-Fixed-Fee
2	DTRA01-01-D-0011/0003	Firm-Fixed-Price
3	DTRA01-01-D-0011/0004	Cost-Plus-Fixed-Fee
4	DTRA01-01-D-0011/0006	Cost-Plus-Fixed-Price
5	DTRA01-01-D-0011/0007	Cost-Plus-Award-Fee
6	DTRA01-01-D-0012/0002	Cost-Plus-Fixed-Fee
7	DTRA01-01-D-0012/0004	Cost-Plus-Award-Fee
8	DTRA01-01-D-0012/0007	Cost-Plus-Fixed-Fee
9	DTRA01-01-D-0012/0008	Cost-Plus-Fixed-Fee
10	DTRA01-01-D-0013/0001	Cost-Plus-Fixed-Fee
11	DTRA01-01-D-0013/0002	Cost-Plus-Award-Fee
12	DTRA01-01-D-0013/0006	Cost-Plus-Fixed-Fee
13	DTRA01-01-D-0013/0009	Cost-Plus-Award-Fee
14	DTRA01-01-D-0013/0013	Cost-Plus-Award-Fee
15	DTRA01-01-D-0014/0001	Cost-Plus-Fixed-Fee/Firm-Fixed-Price

Table C-2. Task Orders with Inadequate Explanation of Type Contract Used

Item Number	Contract/Task Order Number	Contract Type
1	DTRA01-01-D-0010/0001	Cost-Plus-Award-Fee
2	DTRA01-01-D-0010/0002	Cost-Plus-Award-Fee
3	DTRA01-01-D-0011/0004	Cost-Plus-Fixed-Fee
4	DTRA01-01-D-0011/0006	Cost-Plus-Fixed-Fee
5	DTRA01-01-D-0011/0008	Cost-Plus-Fixed-Fee
6	DTRA01-01-D-0011/0009	Cost-Plus-Award-Fee
7	DTRA01-01-D-0012/0002	Cost-Plus-Fixed-Fee
8	DTRA01-01-D-0012/0005	Cost-Plus-Fixed-Fee
9	DTRA01-01-D-0012/0007	Cost-Plus-Fixed-Fee
10	DTRA01-01-D-0012/0008	Cost-Plus-Fixed-Fee
11	DTRA01-01-D-0012/0009	Cost-Plus-Fixed-Fee
12	DTRA01-01-D-0013/0001	Cost-Plus-Fixed-Fee
13	DTRA01-01-D-0013/0002	Cost-Plus-Award-Fee
14	DTRA01-01-D-0013/0005	Cost-Plus-Fixed-Fee
15	DTRA01-01-D-0013/0006	Cost-Plus-Fixed-Fee
16	DTRA01-01-D-0013/0008	Cost-Plus-Fixed-Fee
17	DTRA01-01-D-0013/0009	Cost-Plus-Award-Fee
18	DTRA01-01-D-0013/0010	Cost-Plus-Fixed-Fee
19	DTRA01-01-D-0013/0012	Cost-Plus-Fixed-Fee
20	DTRA01-01-D-0014/0004	Cost-Plus-Fixed-Fee

Appendix D. Report Distribution

Office of the Secretary of Defense

Under Secretary of Defense (Comptroller)/Chief Financial Officer
    Director, Program Analysis and Evaluation
    Deputy Chief Financial Officer
    Deputy Comptroller (Program/Budget)
Under Secretary of Defense for Acquisition, Technology, and Logistics
    Assistant to the Secretary of Defense (Nuclear and Chemical and Biological Defense
        Programs)
        Deputy Assistant to the Secretary of Defense (Chemical Demilitarization and Threat
            Reduction)
    Director, Defense Procurement and Acquisition Policy
Under Secretary of Defense for Policy
    Deputy Under Secretary of Defense (Technology Security Policy and Counter-
        Proliferation)

Department of the Army

Assistant Secretary of the Army (Financial Management and Comptroller)
Auditor General, Department of the Army

Department of the Navy

Naval Inspector General
Auditor General, Department of the Navy

Department of the Air Force

Assistant Secretary of the Air Force (Financial Management and Comptroller)
Auditor General, Department of the Air Force

Combatant Command

Inspector General, U.S. Joint Forces Command

Other Defense Organizations

Director, Defense Threat Reduction Agency

Non-Defense Federal Organizations and Individuals

Office of Management and Budget

Congressional Committees and Subcommittees, Chairman and Ranking Minority Member

Senate Committee on Appropriations
Senate Subcommittee on Defense, Committee on Appropriations
Senate Committee on Armed Services
Senate Committee on Foreign Relations
Senate Committee on Governmental Affairs
House Committee on Appropriations
House Subcommittee on Defense, Committee on Appropriations
House Committee on Armed Services
House Committee on Government Reform
House Subcommittee on Government Efficiency and Financial Management, Committee on Government Reform
House Subcommittee on National Security, Emerging Threats, and International Relations, Committee on Government Reform
House Subcommittee on Technology, Information Policy, Intergovernmental Relations, and the Census, Committee on Government Reform
House Committee on International Relations
House Subcommittee on International Terrorism, Nonproliferation and Human Rights, Committee on International Relations

Defense Threat Reduction Agency Comments

Defense Threat Reduction Agency
8725 John J Kingman Road MS 6201
Ft Belvoir, VA 22060-6201

JUL 29 2004

MEMORANDUM FOR DEPARTMENT OF DEFENSE INSPECTOR GENERAL,
ASSISTANT INSPECTOR GENERAL FOR CONTRACT
MANAGEMENT

SUBJECT: Defense Threat Reduction Agency (DTRA) Comments on Proposed Audit
Report on Contracts Awarded by DTRA in Support of the Cooperative
Threat Reduction Program (Project No. D2003CF-0183)

DTRA extends its appreciation to the audit staff for its work in reviewing task
orders awarded under the DTRA Cooperative Threat Reduction Integrating Contracts.
As requested in your correspondence to us dated May 4, 2004, we offer the attached
comments.

Please contact Mr. Kenneth Harsha, at (703)767-7890, or via e-mail at
Kenneth.harsha@dtra.mil, for additional information.

TRUDY H. CLARK
Maj Gen, USAF
Acting Director

Attachment:
As stated

Defense Threat Reduction Agency (DTRA) Comments on Draft Department of Defense Inspector General (DoD IG) Project No. D2003CF-0183

DTRA's comments to the draft DoD IG report are based on a revised Executive Summary of the report provided electronically to DTRA on July 16, 2004 (Attachment 1). The revised Executive Summary reflects the results of a meeting conducted on July 14, 2004, between the DoD IG and DTRA. The purpose of that meeting was to reconcile factual differences in the draft report and to reach a mutual understanding on issues contained therein. DTRA appreciated this opportunity and acknowledges that the revised Executive Summary is a reflection of a better understanding of the different interpretations of the Federal Acquisition Regulation (FAR) concerning fair opportunity competition requirements and the supporting documentation for multiple award Indefinite Delivery/Indefinite Quantity contracts.

The DoD IG indicated that the remainder of the report will be revised to reflect the July 14, 2004, revision of the Executive Summary.

Finding A. Competition of Task Orders

DTRA is pleased to note the DoD IG found that we effectively use the multiple award process to efficiently streamline Cooperative Threat Reduction (CTR) Program procurements. The CTR Program has numerous unique attributes that require the application of prudent business practices in order to achieve effective competition and still be responsive to the dynamic mission requirements of the program. We believe the process of competing the entire project among all the Cooperative Threat Reduction Integrating Contractors (CTRIC), then systematically and logically issuing separate orders to the successful contractor for integral project phases (i.e., planning/design phase, permit/licensing phase, infrastructure renovation phase, construction phase, etc.) represents a prudent business approach. The separation of some CTR project phases into individual orders has proven to be a successful method of mitigating the unique performance and cost risks associated with contractor performance in countries of the former Soviet Union (FSU). These task orders are issued for a particular phase of the project and are used to identify, analyze, mitigate, track, and control program risks. For example, program risks include uncertainty surrounding the conduct of business in the FSU; complex FSU legal and regulatory environments; unknown site conditions, and the need to secure required host nation commitments before funding the next phase of the project. Phasing of task orders on a project basis also provides leverage to the United States Government in requiring FSU subcontractors to complete their portion of the project prior to moving to the next phase. Another critical benefit of phasing projects is the provision of an exit strategy if problems arise. In fact, a prior DoD IG audit (Project D-2003-131) affirmed phasing as a means to mitigate program risks.

The DoD IG identified that on 3 of the 32 task orders issued under the CTRIC contracts, DTRA did not provide each contractor fair opportunity to be considered for the subsequent phases of a multiple phased project or cite one of the FAR's exceptions to fair opportunity. The nature of the FSU environment, especially licensing and permitting requirements and FSU subcontractor relationships, makes it improbable that another contractor would be able to successfully accomplish work in a follow-on phase. In addition, our actions were based on the fact that all of the CTRIC contractors were afforded an equal opportunity to compete for the entire project with the understanding that there would not likely be opportunities to compete for future phases of the particular project. The order placement procedures of the streamlined approach and the down-select process were developed under the broad discretion granted to the Contracting Officer by FAR Part 16.5 and were published in the original solicitation for establishment of the multiple CTRIC contracts. However, DTRA acknowledges that FAR 16.505 (b) (2) requires that, for all orders over $2,500, every multiple Indefinite Delivery/Indefinite Quantity (IDIQ) awardee must be given a fair opportunity to compete or an exception to fair opportunity must be documented. As noted in Finding A, for all future CTRIC task orders, DTRA will either compete subsequent task orders or will document the rationale for a fair opportunity exception.

Regarding the comments related to the CTRIC award term provisions which were included to incentivize the contractors, award term provisions were allowable at the time of the CTRIC awards and, as noted in your report, did not violate any FAR provision. While we agree the award term provisions contribute to limiting the competitive environment, it is not clear that the limits on competition are as serious as your report suggests. The CTRIC contracts are IDIQ contracts in which the Government's only obligation is to award the minimum quantity. DTRA fully retains the right to award CTR projects to other contractors if circumstances warrant, and indeed, we have done so when such awards were in the best interest of the Government. In addition, although 55 contractors originally expressed interest in the program by attending an early planning Industry Day for the original CTRIC solicitation in 2001, only six proposals were received in response to this solicitation. The majority of the attendees represented firms interested only in subcontracting opportunities, not as a prime integrating contractor.

2

Final Report
Reference   .

Added,
see
Appendix C
Page 23.

Finding B. Contract Documentation

DTRA concurs with Finding B. Focusing more attention on improving documentation will help to avoid inclusion of erroneous accounting and appropriation data on contract actions. DTRA does have internal management controls in place to verify that accounting and appropriation data are properly assigned to a task order. The requiring activity must receive concurrence from DTRA's Comptroller on the purchase request package as a part of the funds certification process. Additionally, the Contracting Officer, prior to signing an award, is responsible for ensuring the accuracy and completeness of accounting and appropriation data.

DTRA has strengthened its internal controls by placing additional oversight responsibility in the majority of our Directorates via the creation of a Senior Business Officer (SBO). SBOs assist in business-related functions including the commitment, obligation, and expenditure of funds. The SBO position in the Cooperative Threat Reduction Directorate had been vacant until July 12, 2004. This additional senior-level oversight, along with existing internal controls, is sufficient to prevent a reoccurrence of the error that contributed to this finding. Additional focus on internal management controls will also help to ensure that our contract file documentation meets all the FAR requirements.

DTRA concurs with the need to focus more attention on improving documentation to ensure that negotiated labor hours, subcontractor pricing, indirect rates and other direct costs are fully supported and explained. The draft audit does not indicate which 15 task orders are in question; however, DTRA has been proactive in expanding the Program Manager's role in proposal evaluations. As an internal control, DTRA published, "A Guide to Preparing Business Clearances" dated June 23, 2003, that provides detailed guidance and samples on how to document analysis of major cost elements in the Price Negotiation Memorandum. The purpose of the Business Clearance Guide is to help Contracting Officers document that a proposed negotiation objective is sound, fully supported, and that the final price is fair and reasonable. The current draft "CTRIC Business Processes and Associated Responsibilities Guide", dated August 2003, clearly requires Program Managers to document their evaluation of contractor proposed labor hours. Page four of the Guide states that, "The TRSC (Threat Reduction Support Center)[1] cost estimators will perform a detailed evaluation of the contractor's cost proposal. This evaluation will examine all major cost elements, which will be addressed in the evaluation report."

---

[1] TRSC provides program support services to the CT Program Office.

3

DTRA concurs with the need to focus additional attention on documenting the justification for the contract type selection. While our current process of Early Strategy Sessions (ESS) provides the appropriate venue to review the reasons for selecting a certain contract type, our files may not have adequately documented these discussions. The guidance provided under the Recommended Acquisition Strategy section of enclosure A (Sample ESS Slides) of the draft Guide requires that the contract type selected and the accompanying rationale be documented. The draft Guide requires the CTRIC Support Team to prepare a draft memorandum for record of the ESS proceedings, coordinate it with the ESS participants, and file the final version signed by the program manager in the Task Order Requirements Package (TORP). The TORP, including the ESS slides, is then submitted to the contracting office, to become a part of the official contract file. In addition to the aforementioned Guide, DTRA's "Guide to Preparing Business Clearances", dated June 23, 2003, requires the Contracting Officer to document in Price Negotiation Memorandums why a particular contract type was selected.

DTRA also employs extensive and independent reviews by the Contracts Policy Oversight and Career Management Branch and the General Counsel's office prior to award of a task order to ensure compliance with all policies and regulations. The Contracting Officer will ensure that the Program Managers are adhering to the internal controls that are in place regarding complete and well-documented analyses of proposed labor hours and will provide justification for the type of contract selected.

We agree with the recommendation to finalize the Cooperative Threat Reduction Integrating Contract Business Processes and Associated Responsibilities guidance document. A completed and implemented guidance document will be finalized and implemented over the next several months.

4

Team Members

The Office of the Deputy Inspector General for Auditing of the Department of Defense, Contract Management prepared this report. Personnel of the Office of the Inspector General of the Department of Defense who contributed to the report are listed below.

Terry L. McKinney
Timothy E. Moore
Robert E. Bender
Steven I. Case
Cheryl L. Snyder
Karen A. Ulatowski
David P. Goodykoontz
Kevin G. Burrowes
Breon E. Dehoux
Theresa L. Tameris